WISDOM
of the
JEWISH SAGES

WISDOM
of the
JEWISH SAGES

A Modern Reading of *Pirke Avot*

RABBI RAMI M. SHAPIRO

BELL TOWER • NEW YORK

Copyright © 1993 by Rami M. Shapiro

Published by Bell Tower, an imprint of Harmony Books, a division
of Crown Publishers, Inc., 201 East 50th Street, New York, New
York 10022. Member of the Crown Publishing Group.

Random House, Inc. New York, Toronto, London, Sydney,
Auckland.

Originally published as *Teachings: Reflections on Pirke Avot* by Light
House Press, Miami, Florida, in 1993.

Bell Tower and colophon are trademarks of Crown Publishers, Inc.

Manufactured in the United States of America

Design by M. Kristen Bearse

Library of Congress Cataloging-in-Publication Data
Mishnah. Avot. English.
    Wisdom of the Jewish sages: a modern reading of *pirke
avot*/Rami M. Shapiro.
        Originally published: *Teachings.* Miami, Fla.: Light House
        Press, 1993.
        I. Shapiro, Rami M.   II. Title.
BM506.A2E5   1995
296.1'23—dc20   94-20922
                                                                       CIP

ISBN 0-517-79966-9
1 0 9 8 7 6

CONTENTS

PREFACE   VII

CHAPTER ONE   I

CHAPTER TWO   21

CHAPTER THREE   43

CHAPTER FOUR   67

CHAPTER FIVE   97

CHAPTER SIX   125

EPILOGUE   139

PREFACE

Pirke Avot (pronounced peer-kay ah-vote) is a collection of rabbinic sayings compiled sometime between the years 250 and 275 of the Common Era, although the Sages cited in the text lived much earlier.

Simon the Righteous, the first of sixty-five authorities quoted, taught during the third century B.C.E. and the last of these rabbis lived during the middle of the third century C.E.

Pirke Avot was transmitted and eventually recorded in Hebrew (with some passages in Aramaic). Over the centuries it has become the principal ethical scripture for Jews. As one Jewish proverb puts it: "One who wishes to attain piety and virtue should turn to the *Pirke Avot*."

I have turned and returned to this brief and powerful collection for more than fifteen years. It has never failed to instruct me in the simple truths of everyday living. No matter how familiar the passage, its meaning seems to sharpen with each encounter. The sayings of these ancient Jewish Sages address me each time as if for the first time—which, of course, is the nature of true revelation.

Revelation is that Truth about Reality that arises when we take our place in the world. Taking our place in the world means being fully present to and in the moment. All of *Pirke Avot* is devoted to helping us take our place.

Most of us are out of place. We are distracted by the inner chatter that we call "self," "I," and ego. We identify with the noise in our heads and imagine that we are somehow to be found inside ourselves. This is incorrect. There is no "me" separate from the moment and all that is happening in it. I am not other than what is happening now. It is when I open fully to what is happening and cease the mental exertion of separation that I take my place and awaken to the wholeness that is Reality.

Consider a jigsaw puzzle. Each piece has its place and no other piece can fit that place. Yet no one piece makes sense on its own. Each piece needs the whole for its integrity and coherence. And the whole needs each piece to fulfill its purpose and bring meaning and order to the puzzle. Once a piece is in its proper place, its separateness is surrendered. We know a piece is in its place when it blends with the whole and disappears.

What is true for a puzzle is true for Reality, with one exception: There is no hand putting us in our place. We must do that for ourselves. We must discover our place and take it. And when we do this, we discover the integrity and meaning of the whole; we discover the divine energy that flows through all things and links each to the other and all to God. This is why *Pirke Avot* refers to God over and again as *haMakom*, the Place—the Place where you are living at this and every moment.

God, Reality, is not an abstraction; God is the Whole manifest in infinite parts. This is what it means to be created in the image of God. The mission of the individual is to take his or her place in the puzzle by letting go of the illusion of fragmentation and bringing things into harmony with each other. This is what our Sages call *Tikkun haOlam*, the repair of the world.

There is no magical technique for letting go of our sense of separation. There is no method that one can master. Formal meditation, prayer, and yoga all contain the element of self that is at the heart of fragmentation. True meditation, true prayer, and true yoga is one's everyday life lived without hesitation.

In the *V'ahavta* prayer, we Jews are commanded to love God—which can only mean to embrace Reality, for God is Reality—with all our heart, with all our soul, and with all our might. This is the way of true living: to hold nothing back, to put all our heart and soul and physical being into whatever Reality needs us to do.

We are Reality's way of accomplishing Reality's ends. Much of what we are asked to do seems trivial: clean the yard, vacuum the floor, wash the dog, or change the baby. As the Hasidic Sage Schneur Zalman taught: "The purpose of Creation is to reveal the Infinite in the details of the finite." God is in the details, and holiness is doing rightly with full attention. That is true meditation: living with attention one deed at a time.

This English version of *Pirke Avot* is not a translation; it is an interpretive reading. My goal is not to translate Hebrew and Aramaic into English, but to make plain the message of *Avot* as I understand it.

There is nothing definitive about this reading. It is not meant to replace others and may be used in conjunction with them. What I have written here is the address of the Sages as I hear it. Nothing more.

The writing of this book was a labor of love. More than four years went into this reading, trying over and again to find just the right words to release the message (if not the literal meaning) of the Sages. While people are free to criticize my understanding, I trust none will doubt my sincerity.

Love alone, however, does not produce books. Publishing requires inspiration, editorial know-how, and not a little faith. I was blessed in all three of these by my teacher, David Reynolds, my colleague David Cooper, and my editor, Toinette Lippe. It was David Reynolds' teaching of Constructive Living that got this project rolling. It was David Cooper and Toinette who carried it beyond my wildest dreams.

I believe in the wisdom found in these pages. It has shaped my life and continues to do so, as I hope it will shape yours. We all owe a debt of gratitude to those who saw this through. I cannot thank them enough. May they go from strength to strength.

R.M.S.
Passover 5754

Upon Israel,
and upon the Rabbis,
and upon their disciples,
and upon all their disciples,
and upon all who engage in the study of Torah
in this place and every place,
to them and to you—
abundant life, grace, loving kindness, mercy, good work,
and true healing
from the One who addresses us all
moment to moment.

AMEN

CHAPTER ONE

*M*oses received Torah at Sinai
and transmitted it to Joshua;
Joshua passed it to the Elders,
and the Elders to the Prophets;
the Prophets handed it down to the Sages,
who emphasized three things:

Be cautious in judgment.
What passes for Truth
is often only hallowed opinion.

Raise up many students.
Help them see Reality for themselves;
remove dependency—
there is no hierarchy in true learning.

Make a fence for Torah.
Distinguish historical form from timeless Truth;
dare to change the first to uphold the second.

I:I

Shimon the Righteous, one of the last Sages, used to say:

The world stands upon three things—

Upon Reality.
Upon self-emptying prayer and meditation.
Upon acts of love and kindness.

I:2

Antigonus of Sokho received the Teaching
from Shimon the Righteous.
He used to say:

Live without hesitation.
Dwell not on outcome or reward.
Act with full attention.

I:3

Yose ben Yoezer of Tzeredah and
  Yose ben Yochanan of Jerusalem
  received the teaching from
  Shimon the Righteous and Antigonus of Sokho.
  Yose ben Yoezer said:

Make your home a meeting place of the wise.
Cover yourself with the dust of their feet,
taking up their journey for yourself.
Drink their words thirstily
but do not suppose that your thirst
can be quenched vicariously.

   I:4

*Y*ose ben Yochanan of Jerusalem said:

Be hospitable.
Treat the poor as family.
Do not speak idly.

One who speaks without attention
and uses words without care
speaks shallowly,
listens poorly,
gives bad advice,
and falls easily into gossip.
Such inattention causes harm
and dishonors yourself and others.

    I:5

*J*oshua ben Perachya and Nittai of Arbel
received the Teaching from Yose ben Yoezer
and Yose ben Yochanan.
Joshua ben Perachya said:

Find a teacher
to challenge your answers.

Acquire a friend
to challenge your questions.

Allow everyone the room to doubt:
the ability to challenge opinions—
even your own.

    I:6

*N*ittai of Arbel said:

Do not cooperate with a wicked neighbor,
for this destroys community.

Do not collaborate with an evil person,
for this destroys society.

Do not despair because of suffering,
for life is suffering.
Suffering and also joy.
When life brings you suffering, hurt.
When life brings joy, laugh.
Cling to nothing
for all is fleeting.

I:7

*J*udah ben Tabbai and Shimon ben Shetach
received the Teaching from Joshua ben Perachya
and Nittai of Arbel.
Judah ben Tabbai said:

If called upon to judge, do not take sides.
To avoid bias, regard all parties as guilty.
When judgment is accepted,
regard all parties as innocent.

Do not cling to judgments
nor imagine that the good cannot err
or the wicked correct their ways.
All life is change,
all feeling is in flux.
Look to what is now
and act accordingly.

I:8

Shimon ben Shetach said:

When seeking Truth,
question thoughtfully.
Choose your words carefully:
A shrewd listener can detect your bias
and through your words, learn to lie.

The "truths" we desire
support what we already know.
We become victims of our own
opinions and rationalizations.

The Truth we need
frees us from the known,
makes us simple,
and plants us firmly in Reality.

   I:9

Shemaya and Avtalyon received the Teaching from
Judah ben Tabbai and Shimon ben Shetach.
Shemaya said:

Love work.
Constructive labor
is vital to balanced living.

Hate authority. Reality alone is true.
No matter how famous the mouth,
check the words against experience.

Do not become intimate with power.
There is nothing we can control
beyond our own doing.
Relinquish power, embrace Reality,
and do what must be done.

I:10

*A*vtalyon said:

Be careful with words.
C–O–W gives no milk.
M–A–N–U–R–E has no stench.
L–O–V–E knows no passion.
Mistake words for Truth,
and you exile yourself from Reality.
Others may follow and
drink the poison of your confusion.
They will die, and Truth will be defiled.

I:II

*H*illel and Shammai received the Teaching
from Shemaya and Avtalyon.
Hillel said:

Be disciples of Aaron—
loving peace and acting peacefully;
loving people
and drawing them to Reality.

    I:12

*H*illel used to say:

> Pursuing fame is self-destructive;
> it distracts us from Reality and
> focuses our energy on ourselves.
>
> Those who do not increase knowledge
> decrease knowledge.
> But don't mistake knowledge for "talk";
> one who knows acts knowingly.
> Fools talk, and their talk too often fools.
>
> Those who cease to learn cease to live.
> Life is learning—attending to Reality.
> Anything less is the sleepwalk of death.
>
> Those who misuse knowledge shall not endure,
> for only Reality endures.
> If you are not attending to Reality,
> where are you?
>
>   I:13

*H*illel used to say:

If I am not for myself, who will be for me?

If I am only for myself, what am I?

And if not now, when?

I:14

Shammai said:

Attend to Reality diligently.

Say little and do much.

Receive all people with kindness.

I:15

$\mathcal{R}$abban Gamliel said:

Make yourself a Sage.
Rely upon Reality, not authority.

Free yourself from crippling self-consciousness.
Attend to each moment
and act without hesitation.

Do not tithe by guesswork.
Justice is not a matter of whim.
Today you may feel generous;
tomorrow you may feel stingy.
Give what is just because it is just.

I:16

Shimon ben Gamliel said:

I grew up among the Sages.
All my life I listened to their words.
Yet I have found nothing better than silence.

Study is not the goal, doing is.
Do not mistake "talk" for "action."
Pity fills no stomach.
Compassion builds no house.
Understanding is not yet justice.

Whoever multiplies words causes confusion.
The truth that can be spoken
is not the Ultimate Truth.
Ultimate Truth is wordless,
the silence within the silence.
More than the absence of speech,
More than the absence of words,
Ultimate Truth is the seamless being-in-place
that comes with attending to Reality.

I:17

$\mathcal{R}$abban Shimon ben Gamliel said:

The world stands upon three things:

Upon truth.
Upon peace.
Upon justice.

"Speak truth each to the other, establish peace,
and render honest judgment in your gates."
(ZECHARIAH 8:16)

   I:18

CHAPTER TWO

*R*abbi Judah haNassi said:

What is the right path for a person to follow?
One that honors both self and other.

Be attentive in all you do;
do not judge one deed small and another great,
for you cannot always know their significance.

Be virtuous, even if virtue is costly.
Avoid sin, even if sin is profitable.

Remember three things and you will not err:
If your deeds shouldn't be known,
perhaps they shouldn't be done.
If your words shouldn't be shared,
perhaps they shouldn't be spoken.
Act with attention,
for all your deeds have consequence.

II:I

Rabban Gamliel, son of Judah haNassi, said:

Engrossed in study,
engaged in good work,
one forgets selfish desire.

Learning without labor is barren;
it does nothing to better the world.

Labor without learning is empty;
it does nothing to enlighten the world.

If employed by the community,
labor for the people and not for power.

If you carry on the good work of your
predecessors, their merit will sustain you.
Their righteousness will endure through you,
and you will be credited with great success,
as if you had accomplished the task alone.

II:2

Rabban Gamliel also taught:

Be wary of those in power,
for their friendship is often
a matter of convenience.

They appear as friends
when it suits them,
but they will not stand by you
in time of need.

II:3

$\mathcal{R}$abban Gamliel used to say:

Desire only that which has already been given.
Want only that which you already have.

As a river empties into the ocean,
empty yourself into Reality.
When you are emptied into Reality,
you are filled with compassion,
desiring only justice.
When you desire only justice,
the will of Reality becomes your will.
When you are filled with compassion,
there is no self to oppose another
and no other to stand against oneself.

   II:4

*H*illel said:

Do not abandon community.

Do not deceive yourself even unto the day you die.

Do not judge others
until you stand in their place.

Do not gossip or whisper slander,
for in the end, it will be heard.

Do not say, "When I find time, I will study";
time is never found, only made.

II:5

*H*illel would say:

The careless cannot avoid harm,
nor the inattentive become holy.

One too shy to question cannot learn,
nor can the impatient teach.

Those obsessed with business
cannot become wise.

And in a situation filled with cowardice,
strive for courage!

II:6

Once Hillel saw a skull floating in the water.
He said to it:

Because you drowned others,
you were drowned.
And in the end,
those who drowned you
will themselves be drowned.

Our deeds fashion our destiny.
Heaven and Hell are in our own hands.

II:7

*H*illel used to say:

More flesh, more worms.
More things, more anxiety.
More lovers, more illusion.
More maids, more exploitation.
More servants, more robbery.
But . . .
More Torah, more Life.
More learning, more wisdom.
More counsel, more insight.
More charity, more peace.

Acquire a good name, and you acquire fame,
but acquire wisdom, and you acquire eternity,
awakening to Reality
in the timeless moment
of the eternal now.

    II:8

Rabban Yochanan ben Zakkai received the Teaching from Hillel and Shammai.
He used to say:

If people think you are wise,
do not think that you are special.
Wisdom comes from knowing Reality,
and knowing Reality is the purpose
for which you were created.

II:9

Rabban Yochanan ben Zakkai
had five principal disciples:
Rabbi Eliezer ben Horkenos,
Rabbi Joshua ben Chananya,
Rabbi Jose haCohen,
Rabbi Shimon ben Nethanel,
and Rabbi Elazar ben Arach.
He used to list their main qualities:

Eliezer ben Horkenos—a plastered well
that loses not even a drop.

Joshua ben Chananya—kind and gentle;
happy is she who bore him.

Jose haCohen—pious.

Shimon ben Nethanel—careful.

Elazar ben Arach—an ever-renewing spring.

II:10

*R*abban Yochanan used to say:

If all of Israel's Sages
were on one side of a scale
with Eliezer ben Horkenos on the other,
Eliezer would outweigh them all.

Abba Shaul said in Yochanan's name:

If all the Sages of Israel
including Eliezer ben Horkenos
were on one side of a scale
with Elazar ben Arach on the other,
Elazar ben Arach would outweigh them all.

II:11

*R*abbi Yochanan said to his disciples:

Go out and see
which is the right path to follow.

Rabbi Eliezer said: Open the eye to Reality.
Rabbi Joshua: Be a good friend.
Rabbi Jose: Be a good neighbor.
Rabbi Shimon: Master foresight to avoid error.
Rabbi Elazar: Cultivate a kind and gentle heart.

Yochanan said:

I prefer the words of Elazar ben Arach,
for his words include all the other words.

   II:12

Yochanan said to his disciples:

Go out and see
which is the wrong path for a person to follow.

Rabbi Eliezer said: Blind the eye to Reality.
Rabbi Joshua: Be a bad friend.
Rabbi Jose: Be a bad neighbor.
Rabbi Shimon: Borrow without repaying.
Rabbi Elazar: Inure the heart to compassion.

Yochanan said:

I prefer the words of Elazar ben Arach,
for his words include all the other words.

II:13

*Y*ochanan's disciples each taught three things.

Rabbi Eliezer said:

Let the honor of your friend be as your own.
Be not quick to anger.
Attend to Reality one day before you die.

He also said:

Be warmed by the Sages' fire,
but beware the coals—

Mistake words for Reality,
and insight falls to cleverness,
Truth falls to opinion,
and reason becomes rationalization.

The words of the wise are white-hot coals—
burning those who cling to them,
warming those who know
how to keep their distance.

II:14

Rabbi Joshua said:

Greed,
sourness,
and hatred for people
exclude you from the world.

II:15

$\mathcal{R}$abbi Jose said:

Let your friend's possessions
be as dear to you as your own.

Study Torah with full attention—
the scrolls are inherited;
their wisdom must be earned.

Act in accord with virtue,
that all your deeds promote justice.

II:16

Rabbi Shimon said:

Recite the Shema with attention,
for this finger points to Truth:
Hear, O Israel,
the source and substance of all is God,
the source and substance of all is One.

Do not make prayer mechanical.
Let it be a cry for grace and mercy,
that love replace fear
in the place in which you stand.

And do not consider yourself evil.
There is no one without good;
There is no one without evil.
Each moment, you are called upon to choose
what you shall bring into the world.
The choice is yours. So, too, the consequences.

II:17

$\mathcal{R}$abbi Elazar said:

Be attentive in Torah study,
for Torah points to Truth.

Know how to answer the faithless,
sharing what you see
without stealing either their vision
or their blindness.

Know for whom you labor;
you are life's means to accomplish life's ends.

Your employer will pay you
the wages of your work,
and all our deeds have consequence.

Know your purpose
and act from it without hesitation.

II:18

Rabbi Tarfon said:

The day is short.
The task is great.
The workers are lazy.

The stakes are high.
The employer—impatient!

Time is fleeting.
Now is eternal.
Discipline yourself to attention,
for the alternative is despair.

    II:19

*R*abbi Tarfon would say:

You are not obligated to complete the work,
but neither are you free to abandon it.

Do not be daunted
by the enormity of the world's grief.
Do justly, now.
Love mercy, now,
Walk humbly, now.

If you attend to Reality,
you will receive great reward;
for effort itself is good fortune.

Reality can be trusted
to pay you the value of your work;
every deed has a consequence.

And know this—
the payment of the righteous is tranquillity:
knowing that "this, too, shall pass."

    II:20

CHAPTER THREE

Akavya ben Mahalalel said:

Reflect on three things,
and you will not mistake yourself
for someone special:

Whence you come,
where you are going, and
to whom you must give account.

Whence do you come?
From the accidental mixing of egg and sperm.

Where are you going?
To a place of dust, worms, and maggots.

To whom must you give account?
To Reality, the undeceivable One.

III:1

*R*abbi Chanina, the Deputy High Priest, said:

Work to establish a healthy government:
One that protects us from enemies without
and from criminals within;
one that establishes courts of justice
to rule fairly on our disputes.

If it were not for this,
people would swallow each other alive.

   III:2

Rabbi Chananya ben Teradyon said:

If two sit together idly,
sharing no words of Torah or Truth—
this is a company of scorners.
A moment wasted is a moment scorned.

But if two sit together with attention,
sharing words of Torah and Truth,
they are filled with wonder.
A moment of attention is an eternity revealed.
This applies to "two."
What of one? Listen—

"Let one sit alone and be silent,
for God has placed it upon him."
(LAMENTATIONS 3:28)

Alone or in company, Reality is always with us.
Attend to it diligently,
and your mind will open to wisdom
and your heart to understanding.

III:3

*R*abbi Shimon said:

Three who eat together idly,
attending to neither friends nor food
and sharing no words of Torah or Truth—
it is as if they have eaten sacrifices to the dead.
Without attention, there is no life.

But three who eat together mindfully,
attending to talk and taste
and sharing words of Torah and Truth—
it is as if they have dined with God,
for God is Reality and Reality is ever-present.
All we need do is attend.

   III:4

*R*abbi Chanina ben Chachinai said:

Those who stay awake too late at night
neglect the body;

Those who walk alone
neglect the heart;

Those who allow the mind to be idle
neglect the soul.

All these forfeit life—
Even while they live, they are as dead.

III:5

Rabbi Nechunya ben HaKana said:

Whoever accepts the yoke of Torah,
giving of self moment to moment,
must first remove the yoke of power and success,
grasping for self moment to moment.

Whoever removes the yoke of Torah
is chained to the yoke of power and success
and is ultimately crushed
by an avalanche of conceit.

III:6

Rabbi Chalafta ben Dosa said:

A congregation of ten
who sit and share words of Torah and Truth—
Reality is revealed to them: "God stands
in the congregation of the divine." (PSALM 82:1)

This is also true of a band of five:
"God has established his band upon the earth."
(AMOS 9:6)

It is true of three who gather to discern Truth:
"In the midst of judges, God judges." (PSALM 82:1)

It is true of two who speak honestly of Truth:
"They who were mindful of God spoke to each
other, and God listened and heard." (MALACHI 3:16)

It is true even of one who contemplates
the intricacies of Reality
in the silence of the mind: "In every place
where I cause My Name to be remembered,
I will come to you and bless you." (EXODUS 20:24)
And what is God's name if not Reality?

III:7

$\mathcal{R}$abbi Elazar of Barthotha said:

Render unto God what is God's,
for you and all you have are God's.

"All things come from You, and of Your own
have we given You." (I CHRONICLES 29:14)

Everything we are is a gift.
Everything we have is given.

Know whence all things come
and be not dismayed at their passing.

    III:8

Rabbi Jacob said:

If you are walking lost in wonder,
empty of self, and mindful of Reality,
and suddenly you interrupt this peace to exclaim:
"How beautiful is this tree!
How magnificent this field!"
you forfeit life.

The intrusion of self
and the imposing of judgment
separates you from Reality
and snares you in the net of words.

Be still and know.
Embrace it all in silence.

   III:9

*R*abbi Dostai ben Yannai,
in the name of Rabbi Meir, said:

Whoever forgets to attend to life forfeits life:
"Only take heed of yourself
and watch yourself diligently,
lest you forget the things you have seen
with your own eyes." (DEUTERONOMY 4:9)

Can this apply to one who finds attending difficult
and remembering impossible?
Not at all:
"And lest they depart from your heart
all the days of your life." (DEUTERONOMY 4:9)

Life is not forfeited
unless one deliberately refuses
to attend every day of one's life.

   III:10

Rabbi Chanina ben Dosa said:

Those who value right action
over the pursuit of wisdom—
their wisdom endures.

Those who value the pursuit of wisdom
over right action—
their wisdom will not endure.

III:11

*R*abbi Chanina also said:

Those whose deeds
exceed their wisdom—
their wisdom will endure.

Those whose wisdom
exceeds their deeds—
their wisdom will not endure.

III:12

*R*abbi Chanina used to say:

One in whom
everyone delights
Reality delights.

One in whom
everyone takes no delight
Reality takes no delight.

Do not think you can love God
and despise creation.
The two are at root One.

III:13

*R*abbi Dosa ben Harkinas said:

Too much sleep,
too much wine,
too much talk,
and partying with fools
drive you out of the world.

    III:14

Rabbi Elazar of Modin said:

One who profanes the sacred,
exploiting Truth for personal gain;

One who despises the festivals,
mocking the community;

One who humiliates another in public,
causing loss of face and embarrassment;

One who rejects the covenant of Abraham,
abandoning the way of justice;

One who misinterprets Torah,
leading others away from Truth and virtue
—even if learned and charitable—

Such a one forfeits life
and the tranquillity that arises
from attending to Reality.

III:15

Rabbi Ishmael said:

Be cooperative with supervisors.

Be respectful with youth.

Receive all people joyously.

III:16

Rabbi Akiva said:

Sarcasm and silliness
lead a person to bad behavior.

Acting kindly keeps Torah fresh.

Giving justly keeps us from hoarding.

Helping others keeps us from conceit.

Practicing silence keeps us from cleverness.

III:17

Rabbi Akiva used to say:

The preciousness of humanity
as life's self-reflecting mind is only a potential.
We must strive to know: "In the image of God
did God make humankind." (GENESIS 9:6)

The preciousness of people
as children of God is only a potential.
We must come to know:
"You are the children of God."
(DEUTERONOMY 14:1)

The preciousness of Israel
as the bearer of Torah is only a potential.
We must come to know:
"For I give you a good doctrine.
Do not forsake My Torah." (PROVERBS 4:2)

We are life, we are nature, we are God.
It is not enough merely to exist.
We must know our purpose
and do what must be done.

III:18

*R*abbi Akiva used to say:

Everything is foreseen but free choice is given.
Habits predispose us to foregone conclusions,
but we can control our habits.

The world is judged according to goodness.
Despite the evil one sees,
measure life's worth according to its blessings.

And everything is measured according to deeds.
Deeds, not feelings.
Deeds, not intent.
Deeds, not results.
Doing itself is good fortune.

   III:19

$\mathcal{R}$abbi Akiva used to say:

Everything is given on pledge,
a net is cast over all the living.
The store is open, and the merchant gives credit;
the ledger is open, and the hand writes;
whoever wishes to borrow may borrow.
The collectors make their rounds daily
and collect from us whether we know it or not.
They have grounds for what they do,
and the judgment is true.
And everything is ready for the meal.

We are given life that we might enhance life.
Reality allows us to do as we will, good or evil.
And each has its consequence.
Lived justly with compassion,
integrity, and attention,
life is a banquet—sometimes bitter, often sweet—
and none need ever go hungry.

   III:20

*R*abbi Elazar ben Azariah said:

Without Torah, there is no proper conduct.
Without proper conduct, there is no Torah.

Without wisdom, there is no wonder.
Without wonder, there is no wisdom.

Without understanding, there is no knowledge.
Without knowledge, there is no understanding.

Without flour, there is no Torah.
Without Torah, there is no flour.
Only labor and learning together
produce purposeful life.

III:21

*R*abbi Elazar used to say:

Like trees with many branches but few roots
are those whose wisdom exceeds their deeds.
The winds come and easily uproot them.

Like trees with few branches and many roots
are those whose deeds exceed their wisdom.

All the winds in the world can blow against them,
and they will not yield.

III:22

*R*abbi Eleazar Chisma said:

No deed is minor
to one who attends to Reality.

No learning is useless
to one who lives with fullness of mind.

Nothing is beneath doing
to one who knows what needs to be done.

The wise may not achieve fame,
but their days are rich with meaning.

III:23

CHAPTER FOUR

*B*en Zoma said:

Who is wise? One who learns from all:
"From all my teachers I gained insight."
(PSALM 119:99)

Who is strong? One who controls the self:
"Better to have self-control
than to conquer a city." (PROVERBS 16:32)

Who is rich? One who desires only what is given:
"When you eat the fruit of your labors,
be happy and it shall be well with you."
(PSALM 128:2)

Who is honored? One who honors humanity:
"For I honor those who honor Me,
but those who spurn Me shall be dishonored."
(I SAMUEL 29:30)

IV:1

*B*en Azzai said:

Hasten to do even a small deed
and flee from illusion;
for action generates more action,
while wishing generates only frustration.

We are here to act.
We are life's way of getting things done.

The reward for action?
The opportunity to do more.

The payment for illusion?
Despair.

   IV:2

Ben Azzai used to say:

Do not despise anyone.
Do not regard anything as impossible.
There is no one without his hour.
There is no thing without its place.

IV:3

*R*abbi Levitas of Yavneh said:

Be exceedingly humble,
for the hope of humankind
is the worm.

IV:4

Rabbi Yochanan ben Beroka said:

One who ignores Reality,
wandering without attention,
lost in self and unconscious of the world,
will be exposed in public.

It cannot be helped:
Unless you attend to Reality,
you will stumble on the path.
As you stumble along for all to see,
your inattention is visible to the world.

Whether one does so
unconsciously or consciously,
it is all the same
when it comes to ignoring Reality.

IV:5

Rabbi Ishmael ben Rabbi Yose said:

One who learns in order to teach
will be granted the opportunity
both to learn and teach.

One who learns in order to do
will be granted
not only the opportunity to learn and teach,
but also the opportunity to do and be fulfilled.

IV:6

*R*abbi Zadok said:

Do not separate yourself from the community.
In the role of judge, do not act as counsel.

Do not use your knowledge
to exploit others for your personal gain;
do not make of Torah a spade with which to dig.

As Rabbi Hillel taught:
One who exploits learning forfeits life,
for living virtuously
is never at the expense of others.

From this we learn
that those who profit materially from Torah
remove themselves from this world.

IV:7

*R*abbi Yose said:

Whoever honors Truth,
humanity will honor.

Whoever dishonors Truth,
humanity will dishonor.

IV:8

Rabbi Ishmael ben Yose said:

One who does not judge
nor meanspiritedly compare self against others
rids the self of hatred, robbery,
and vain pursuits.

One who is quick to judge
and forever jealous
is foolish, evil,
and filled with pride.

IV:9

Rabbi Ishmael used to say:

Do not judge alone,
for you are too easily blinded by opinion.

There is only One who can judge alone,
and that One never judges,
insisting instead upon Reality
and the consequences of our actions.

And do not say: "Accept my opinion,"
for the power of choice belongs to the people
and not to you.

Only point to the Real and its consequences
and let others engage It as they will.

IV:10

Rabbi Jonathan said:

Whoever attends to Reality when poor
will attend to it when rich.

Whoever ignores Reality when rich
will ignore it when poor.

IV:11

Rabbi Meir said:

Keep your business dealings in perspective
and occupy yourself with Reality.
Be humble before everyone.

If you ignore Reality,
you will be ignored.

If you labor in Reality,
Reality itself will reward you.

What is the reward of Reality?
Living without illusion.

IV:12

Rabbi Eliezar ben Jacob said:

One who performs even one righteous deed
creates a habit of holiness and attention.

One who commits even one sin
begins a habit of selfishness and inattention.

Admitting our errors and attending to Reality
shield us against the calamity of harmful habits.

IV:13

$\mathcal{R}$abbi Yochanan the Sandalmaker said:

Every assembly
that gathers to discern the Truth
will endure,
even if the Truth is not found.

Any assembly
that gathers to further delusion
will not endure,
even if the Truth is found.

IV:14

$\mathcal{R}$abbi Elazar ben Shammua said:

Teachers!
Let the honor of your students
be as precious to you as your own.

Friends!
Let the honor of your friend
be as the honor due your teacher.

Students!
Let the reverence for your teacher
be as dear to you as the awe you sense
when contemplating the heavens.

   IV:15

*R*abbi Judah said:

Be diligent in study.
To learn below your potential
is a betrayal of self
and an insult to life.

IV:16

$\mathcal{R}$abbi Shimon said:

There are three crowns to which people aspire:

The crown of Torah scholarship
comes with a quick mind and a sound memory.

The crown of priesthood
comes with birth into the tribe of Levi.

The crown of royalty
comes with royal birth or the seizing of power.

But a good name transcends them all,
for it is open to all.

IV:17

*R*abbi Nehorai said:

Seek out a place of Torah,
where companions struggle together
in the pursuit of Truth.

Do not presume Torah will come to you;
you must go to her.

Ignorance is as natural as wisdom,
and the difference between them is not always clear.

Do not rely solely on your own understanding,
for there is no one easier to fool than yourself.

Do not rely solely on authority
nor be content with hallowed opinion,
for authority serves only authority.

Only attend to Reality
with fullness of mind, heart, and action
and experience what *is* for yourself.

IV:18

$\mathcal{R}$abbi Yannai said:

It is not within our grasp to explain
the prosperity of the wicked
or the suffering of the righteous.
All we are called upon to do
is to act justly ourselves.

Reality is more complex than we would like.
If we insist upon it making sense,
we will find ourselves despairing.
Reality cannot be neatly packaged,
bound with the ribbon of morality.
Reality is greater than our ideas of good and evil;
Reality is beyond our right and wrong.
Reality is all that is, and this is often at odds
with what we imagine it should be.

Where we can stand up for justice, let us act.
Where we are confounded by Truth,
let us keep silent.

IV:19

*R*abbi Mathya ben Charash said:

Be the first to greet another.

Be a tail among lions
rather than a head among foxes.

  IV:20

$\mathcal{R}$abbi Jacob said:

This world of seemingly separate selves
is like an antechamber
to the world of ultimate unity.

Prepare yourself in the antechamber
so that you will be able to enter the banquet hall.

This world of half-glimpsed Reality
is only a shadow of the world we see
when we fully attend to Reality.

If you would taste the wonder of the Real,
you must attend to this moment here and now.
The banquet is all around you;
if you find you are spiritually hungry,
it is because you refuse to notice the buffet.

   IV:21

*R*abbi Jacob used to say:

Better a single moment of awakening in this world
than eternity in the world to come.

And better a single moment of inner peace
in the world to come than eternity in this world.

Why?
A single moment of awakening in this world
is eternity in the world to come.

The inner peace of the world to come
is living in this world with full attention.

The two are one, flip sides of a coin
forever tumbling and never caught.

IV:22

Rabbi Shimon ben Eleazar said:

Do not seek to calm angry friends
at the height of their anger.
Honor the heat of feeling
by giving it time to cool.

Do not comfort grieving friends
while their dead lie before them.
Honor the shock of grief
by giving it time to find its voice.

Do not question a friend's integrity
in the midst of making a vow.
Honor the sincerity of the moment
by giving it time to flourish or fail.

Do not seek out friends
in the moment of their humiliation.
Honor the pain of embarrassment
by giving it time to fade.

IV:23

*S*amuel the Younger said:

When your enemy falls,
do not rejoice.
When your enemy stumbles,
do not be glad.

Your glee will corrupt you,
your ego will trick you into thinking
that you are different from him.
You will excuse your evil,
and your fate will be as hers.

One who rejoices at another's hurt
is an enemy of all.

IV:24

*E*lisha ben Abuyah said:

Those who learn with an open mind—
to what can they be compared?
To ink written on fresh paper.

Those who learn with a cynic's mind—
to what can they be compared?
To ink written on used paper.
True learning requires fresh paper mind.

Clinging neither to the known nor the unknown,
holding neither to past nor future,
the mind is fresh,
the paper clean
and eager to absorb the ink of the Real.

IV:25

Rabbi Yose ben Judah
of Kefar haBavli said:

Those who learn from beginners—
to what can they be compared?

To those who eat unripe grapes
and drink fresh wine.

Those who learn from masters—
to what can they be compared?

To those who eat ripe grapes
and drink vintage wine.

IV:26

*R*abbi Meir said:

Do not look at the bottle
but at what it contains.

There may be a new jug
filled with old wine
and an old jug
that does not even contain wine.

IV:27

Rabbi Eliezar haKappar said:

Envy, lust, and thirst for honor
drive a person into the self
and out of the world.

IV:28

*R*abbi Eliezar haKappar used to say:

Those who are born are destined to die.
Those who die are destined to return.
Those who live are destined to be judged.

With Reality, there is no wrong,
no forgetting, no bias, no bribe.
All is as it must be; there is no escape.

Despite your wishes, you were conceived.
Despite your wishes, you were born.
Despite your wishes, you live.
Despite your wishes, you die.
Despite your wishes, you are destined
to deal with the consequences of your actions.
So get on with it.

IV:29

CHAPTER FIVE

The world was created by uttering ten phrases.
Why ten, when it could have been
created through one?

To make clear
that there is nothing apart from Reality:
no detail too small as to be unworthy of attention.

This clarity makes possible
the wicked ones' retribution
and the righteous ones' reward.

The wicked deny Reality
and defile their own home.
Their punishment is fear of the world.

The righteous attend to Reality
and establish holiness.
Their reward is equanimity in the world.

   V:I

*F*rom Adam to Noah, there were ten generations.
From the creation of humanity to its destruction,
there were ten generations.
Why?
To teach us the value of patience.

Each generation from Adam to Noah
violated the Truth it had been shown.
Yet no reaction was forthcoming until the tenth.

Reality waits for us to return to Truth.
But continued violation
reaches a point of no return.
Creation and civilization both collapse into chaos.

V:2

*F*rom Noah to Abraham, there were ten generations.
From the destruction of humanity
to its redirection,
there were ten generations.
Why?
To teach us the value of patience.

Each generation from Noah to Abraham
violated the Truth it had been shown.
Yet no reaction was forthcoming until the tenth.

There is no block to turning
other than the habit of our own delusion.
At any time we may choose holiness,
establish justice, spread compassion,
and thus receive the reward of attending to Reality:
a healthy and nurturing world.

V:3

*T*en trials were inflicted upon Abraham,
and he withstood them all.
Why?
To show how great was his commitment.

Suffering is the stuff of life,
and through suffering
one opens the heart to compassion,
the shared pain of living beings.

We withstand our trials
by feeling the pain without abandoning the world.

Suffering without bitterness,
we do justly, even in the face of unjust adversity.

V:4

*T*en wonders were done for our ancestors in Egypt,
and ten at the Sea.

What was their merit
that wonders were done on their behalf?

We do not merit wonder.
We simply open our eyes to it.

Wonder is the heart of life,
beating in the breast of the living.

Do not imagine that you merit wonder—
only dare to encounter it.

V:5

Ten plagues fell upon the Egyptians in Egypt,
and ten at the Sea.
What was their sin that this was done?

The perversion of justice,
the enslaving of others,
the worship of delusion,
the violation of holiness.

Such deeds attract chaos,
uproot mercy,
drive out friendship,
and plunge the world into darkness.

V:6

$\mathcal{T}$en times did our ancestors test Reality:
"They have tested me ten times
and have not listened to My voice."
(NUMBERS 14:22)

What is it to test Reality?
To work against holiness:
to fail to hear the cry of justice,
to refuse to listen to words of wisdom.

Life is forever whispering its secrets:
justice, love, compassion,
the greater unity within and beyond all diversity.

We are too busy to listen,
too noisy to hear anything
but our own foolishness.

Be silent. Be still. Listen and attend.

V:7

*T*en miracles occurred in the Temple:
  the aroma of sacrifice caused no miscarriages;
  no sacrifice ever spoiled;
  no fly was ever found in the slaughterhouse;
  the High Priest was never unclean on Yom Kippur;
  the rain never doused the altar fire;
  no wind ever dispersed the altar smoke;
  the *Omer*, loaves, and showbread had no defect;
  the people stood pressed together
  but had ample room to bow;
  no snake or scorpion ever struck in Jerusalem;
  no one ever said to another: "There is no room
  in which to spend the night in Jerusalem."

Miracles are the ordinary
revealed in their simple splendor.
The Temple was a place of miracles
for it was the place devoted to attending
to the wonder of the ordinary.
Where is that place in your life?
Why is it not here?

  V:8

*T*en things were created at twilight on Sabbath eve:
the mouth of the earth (NUMBERS 16:32),
the mouth of the well (NUMBERS 21:16–18),
the mouth of the ass (NUMBERS 22:28),
the rainbow (GENESIS 9:13),
the *manna* (EXODUS 16:15),
the rod of Moses (EXODUS 4:17),
the *shamir*, the stone-eating worm (I KINGS 6:7, 16),
the Hebrew *alephbet*,
writing, and the Ten Commandments.

And some say also:
the destructive forces of nature,
the hidden grave of Moses (DEUTERONOMY 34:6),
and the ram of Abraham (GENESIS 22:13).

And some say also:
the pliers with which pliers were made—
the archetypal forms of all creation.

V:9

There are seven characteristics of boors
and seven of Sages.

Sages do not speak before those
whose wisdom and experience exceed their own;
do not interrupt another's words;
are not in a hurry to reply;
ask relevant questions, give relevant answers;
speak without deception;
feel free to say, "I don't know"
when the matter is unfamiliar;
acknowledge the Truth and admit error.

The boor is marked by the opposite of these.

V:10

*S*even misdeeds bring their own misfortune:

Robbing the poor of tithes brings famine.

Horrific crimes and violating nature
bring plague.

Perverting justice and Truth brings war.

Spreading false teachings brings chaos.

Idolatry, lust, violence,
and the exploitation of nature
bring exile.

V:11

*A*t four periods does disease increase:
in the fourth year, in the seventh,
at the conclusion of the seventh year,
and at the conclusion of Sukkot.

In the fourth year, if we neglect
the tithe to the poor during the third year;
In the seventh year, if we neglect
the tithe to the poor during the sixth year;
At the conclusion of the seventh year,
if we neglect the law
and let not the poor eat of the fields
during the sabbatical year;
At the conclusion of Sukkot,
if we rob the poor of their portion of the harvest.

Do not imagine you can thrive
at the expense of others:
Injustice to the least undermines the health of all.

V:12

$\mathcal{T}$here are four kinds of people.

There are those who say,
"What's mine is mine, and what's yours is yours."
These are average people, though some say
they are like the people of Sodom.

There are those who say,
"What's mine is yours, and what's yours is mine."
These are boors.

There are those who say,
"What's mine is yours, and what's yours is yours."
These are pious.

There are those who say,
"What's mine is mine, and what's yours is mine."
These are wicked.

V:13

*T*here are four kinds of temperament:

Easy to anger, easy to calm—
the negative is canceled by the positive.

Hard to anger, hard to calm—
the positive is canceled by the negative.

Hard to anger, easy to calm—
such people are truly holy.

Easy to anger, hard to calm—
such people are truly wicked.

V:14

There are four kinds of learners:

Quick to grasp, quick to forget—
gain is canceled by the loss.

Slow to grasp, slow to forget—
loss is canceled by the gain.

Quick to grasp, slow to forget—
a Sage.

Slow to grasp, quick to forget—
the worst learner of all.

V:15

*T*here are four attitudes
   among those who give charity:

Those who give
   but wish that others did not give—
   these covet what belongs to others.

Those who do not give
   but wish others would give—
   these hoard what belongs to themselves.

Those who give and wish others would give—
   these are truly holy.

Those who do not give
   and wish others would not give—
   these are truly wicked.

   V:16

*T*here are four attitudes
relating to the House of Study:

Those who go
but do not live what they learn—
these get credit for going.

Those who live what they learned
but no longer go—
these get credit for doing.

Those who go and do—
these are truly holy.

Those who neither go nor do—
these are truly wicked.

V:17

There are four types
  among those who sit before the Sages:
  sponges, funnels, strainers, and sieves.

Sponges—these absorb everything.

Funnels—these take it all in at one end
and let it all out at the other.

Strainers—these let the wine out
and retain the sediment.

Sieves—these let out the dust
and keep the flour.

   V:18

*L*ove that is contingent
upon something else,
when that something is gone,
love is gone.

Love that is contingent upon nothing,
such a love will never end.

What is an example of contingent love?
The love between Amnon and Tamar,
for Amnon loved her beauty
but did not respect her person.

What is an example of uncontingent love?
The love between David and Jonathan.
For even as they were rivals for the throne,
their love for each other survived.

    V:19

*E*very dispute for the sake of Truth
will in the end prove constructive.

Every dispute not for the sake of Truth
will in the end prove destructive.

What is a dispute for the sake of Truth?
That between Hillel and Shammai,
for though they argued,
their only aim was to reveal the Truth.

What is a dispute not for the sake of Truth?
That between Korach and his followers,
for they argued not for Truth, but for power;
not for the sake of the people
eager to know Reality,
but for themselves
and their hunger to rule over others.

V:20

One who leads the community
toward virtue never causes sin.

One who leads the community
toward sin nevers finds virtue.

Moses was virtuous
and never led the community to sin;
therefore the virtue of the community
was credited to him. (DEUTERONOMY 33:21)

Jeroboam ben Nevat sinned
and led the people to sin;
therefore the sin of the people
is credited to him. (I KINGS 15:30)

V:21

*T*hree traits make one a disciple of Abraham.
Three others make one a disciple of Bil'am.

A discerning eye,
a humble heart,
a tranquil spirit—
these are the traits of Abraham.

A foolish eye,
a lustful heart,
an arrogant spirit—
these are the traits of Bil'am.

The disciples of Abraham eat of this world
and inherit tranquillity.

The disciples of Bil'am hunger in this world
and inherit confusion.

V:22

*J*udah ben Tema said:

Be strong as a leopard,
light as an eagle,
swift as a deer,
and brave as a lion
when carrying out the tasks of righteousness.

V:23

*J*udah ben Tema used to say:

One who hardens his face against the world
is trapped within the self,
closed to Reality,
and lost in a land of
exiled selves and selfishness.

One who softens her face before the world
forgets the self,
is open to Reality,
and creates a world of compassion and peace,
where each is a part of everyone
and everyone a part of all.

V:24

*J*udah ben Tema used to say:

Five is the age to begin to study scripture,
ten to study Mishnah,
thirteen to undertake *mitzvot*, righteous deeds,
fifteen to study Talmud,
eighteen to marry,
twenty to start a career,
thirty to attain full strength,
forty to acquire experience,
fifty to give counsel,
sixty to attain intellectual maturity,
seventy to provide communal leadership,
eighty to reach spiritual strength,
ninety to come to humble renunciation,
one hundred to accomplish perfect grace—
having passed beyond clinging to this world.

V:25

*B*en Bag Bag said:

Turn it and turn it
for everything is in it,
and through it comes clarity of mind.

Grow old and gray in it
and from it do not depart,
for there is no better work than this.

And what is it? Torah, Truth,
the shifting moments of everyday Reality.

Attend to these and live,
even unto the last beating of the heart.

Ignore them and die,
even while the heart beats strongly.

V:26

Ben Hei Hei said:

Effort is its own reward.

We are here to do.
And through doing to learn;
and through learning to know;
and through knowing to experience wonder;
and through wonder to attain wisdom;
and through wisdom to find simplicity;
and through simplicity to give attention;
and through attention
to see what needs to be done. . . .

V:27

CHAPTER SIX

*R*abbi Meir said:

Attend to Reality for its own sake,
for attention itself sustains creation.

The wise are called friend, lover, joy-bringer.
Clothed with humility, avoiding evil,
embracing virtue, they lend good counsel,
sound wisdom, insight, and strength.

Through attention to Reality
comes self-control and discernment.
Secrets are revealed, and
one becomes an ever-fresh spring of wisdom.

The Sage is honored above all others
and yet remains modest, patient, and forgiving.

VI:I

Rabbi Joshua ben Levi said:

Every moment, a voice from Heaven
resounds from Mount Horeb:

Woe to those who disregard Torah,
for they lack insight, act unjustly,
and exile themselves from holiness.

All who practice Torah,
attending to life and revealing Truth,
will be exalted.
Taking up the path of justice and compassion,
they lift up the world
and thus are themselves uplifted.

    VI:2

One who learns from a person
one chapter, one law, one verse,
one expression, or one letter
must treat that person with honor.

King David learned
only two words from Ahithophel
and yet called him
"my equal, my guide, my beloved." (PSALMS 55:14)
If the King of Israel acted thus,
how much more must we honor
even the least of our teachers.

Honor comes through Torah,
for Torah teaches us to honor both self and other.
Good comes through Torah,
for Torah teaches the way of justice,
compassion, and humility.

VI:3

*T*his is the way of Torah,
   the way of attending to Reality:

To eat simply.
To drink even water moderately.
To sleep soundly, even if on the ground.
To endure hardships with grace and humor.
To be ever attentive.

Do this, and tranquillity will be yours.
You will grieve in times of mourning
and rejoice in times of celebration.
You will allow each moment its due
and each task its effort.
You will accept the transience of life
and cease to cling either to suffering or joy.

   VI:4

Do not seek self-aggrandizement
    nor covet fame.
    Let your deeds exceed your learning.

    Do not crave the table of power,
    for the table of wisdom is bigger still;
    the crown of the wise is greater
    than the diadem of kings.

    Reality can be trusted
    to pay the reward for your work—
    for all our deeds have consequence.

    VI:5

Becoming a Sage is more difficult
than becoming a priest or even a king.

Kingship requires thirty qualifications
and priesthood twenty-four,
but the way of Torah requires forty-eight:

Learning, attention, clarity of mind and tongue,
an intuitive heart, awe, reverence, humility, joy,
simplicity, apprenticeship to Sages,
friendship with colleagues, challenging students,
calm deliberation,
knowledge of scripture and Mishnah,
balance in business, worldly affairs,
and sexual intimacy,
sufficient sleep,
avoiding gossip, maintaining humor,
slow to anger, with a gentle heart,
trusting the Sages, accepting suffering,
knowing one's calling, rejoicing in one's portion,
guarding one's words,
not claiming merit for oneself,
being loved,

loving God, humanity, charity, and reproof,
not seeking out honors,
not boasting of one's education,
being loath to judge,
sharing the burdens of others,
giving people the benefit of doubt,
leading others to truth and to peace,
being meticulous in study,
asking probing questions,
answering queries honestly,
listening and discussing,
learning in order to teach and practice,
honing one's teacher's wisdom with questions,
contemplation,
giving credit to those who taught one—
whoever credits a teaching to its author
brings redemption to the world.

  VI:6

*G*reat is Torah,
  calling us to attend to Reality
  in this world and in the world to come.

In this world, through justice and compassion.
In the world to come,
through openness to life's greater unity.

In this world,
by teaching us to attend here and now.
In the world to come,
by teaching us to attend here and now.

All worlds are present here;
all time is present now.
When attending to the moment,
there is no division.

Inattention divides now from then, causing
division, isolation, clinging, and despair.

  VI:7

Rabbi Shimon ben Judah said
in the name of Shimon ben Yohai:

Beauty, strength, riches,
honor, wisdom, old age,
gray hair, and children befit the righteous
and are becoming to the world.
These will come in their time.
So, too, their opposites.

Do not anticipate the one nor cling to the other,
but allow each to rise and fall of its own accord.
In this way the righteous become wise,
the wise become simple,
the simple become ordinary,
and the ordinary become fulfilled.

VI:8

*R*abbi Yose ben Kisma said:

Once when I was walking, I met a man
who offered me a lucrative position in his town.
I said, "Even if you were to give me
all the world's wealth, I would not live elsewhere
than in a place of Torah."

A place without Torah
is a place lost to justice and compassion,
a place confused by inattention,
a place without good deeds.

When we die, nothing accompanies us
but our insight and good deeds.
While we live, these sustain us.

Do not choose to live in a place without honor,
but if you find yourself there,
strive to be honorable.

VI:9

*F*ive things lead to the Holy One:
    Torah—the teaching of wisdom;
    heaven and earth—
    the daily reality of ordinary living;
    Abraham and Sarah—
    the parents of all who seek the Truth;
    Israel—all those who wrestle with the ultimate;
    the Temple—the ever-present place of God.

    VI:10

*E*verything that God,
the source and substance of all,
creates in this world
flows naturally from the essence
of God's divine nature.

Creation is not a choice
but a necessity.
It is God's nature
to unfold time and space.

Creation is the extension of God.
Creation is God encountered in time and space.
Creation is the infinite in the garb of the finite.

To attend to creation is to attend to God.
To attend to the moment is to attend to eternity.
To attend to the part is to attend to the whole.
To attend to Reality is to live constructively.

VI:11

EPILOGUE

Rabbi Chananya ben Akashya said:

Reality is infinite. The infinite includes the finite.
For the finite to know the infinite,
Reality fashions the human mind.

To cultivate that mind, Reality reveals Truth,
pointing the finite back to the infinite.

To bring Truth to humankind,
Reality creates Sages
who carry it into the world.
The Sages of Israel carry it as Torah.

To carry Torah into the world,
The Sages ordain *mitzvot:*
Do justly, love mercy, walk humbly.
Mitzvot and Torah are the gifts of Reality
given to the world through the Sages of Israel.
We honor the gift by living it ourselves.

ABOUT THE AUTHOR

$\mathcal{R}$ami Shapiro, rabbi and storyteller of Temple Beth Or in Miami, Florida, is an award-winning poet and essayist, whose liturgical poems are used in prayer services throughout North America. He has published more than a dozen books of poetry, liturgy, stories, and nonfiction. Rabbi Shapiro holds a doctoral degree in religious studies and lectures widely on contemporary Jewish spirituality. He is the director of the Rasheit Institute for Jewish Spirituality in Miami, where he lives with his wife, son, and two dogs. He spends whatever free time he has communing with his teachers: Martin Buber, Dogen, Ralph Waldo Emerson, Alan Watts, and Krishnamurti.

OTHER BELL TOWER BOOKS

Books that nourish the soul, illuminate the mind,
and speak directly to the heart

Being Home: A Book of Meditations
by Gunilla Norris
An exquisite modern book of hours,
a celebration of mindfulness in everyday activities.
Hardcover 0-517-58159-0 1991

Nourishing Wisdom: A Mind/Body Approach
to Nutrition and Well-Being
by Marc David
A book that advocates awareness in eating.
Hardcover 0-517-57636-8 1991
Softcover 0-517-88129-2 1994

Sanctuaries: The Northeast
A Guide to Lodgings in Monasteries, Abbeys, & Retreats of the U.S.
by Jack and Marcia Kelly
The first in a series of regional guides for those in search of
renewal and a little peace.
Softcover 0-517-57727-5 1991

Grace Unfolding: Psychotherapy in the Spirit of the Tao-te ching
by Greg Johanson and Ron Kurtz
The interaction of client and therapist illuminated through the
gentle power and wisdom of the ancient Chinese classic.
Hardcover 0-517-58449-2 1991
Softcover 0-517-88130-6 1994

**Self-Reliance: The Wisdom of Ralph Waldo Emerson
as Inspiration for Daily Living**
*Selected and with an introduction
by Richard Whelan*
A distillation of Emerson's essential spiritual writings
for contemporary readers.
Softcover 0-517-58512-X 1991

Compassion in Action: Setting Out on the Path of Service
by Ram Dass and Mirabai Bush
Heartfelt encouragement and advice for those ready to commit
time and energy to relieving suffering in the world.
Softcover 0-517-57635-X 1992

**Letters from a Wild State:
Rediscovering Our True Relationship to Nature**
by James G. Cowan
A luminous interpretation of Aboriginal spiritual experience
applied to the leading issue of our time: the care of the earth.
Hardcover 0-517-58770-X 1992

**Silence, Simplicity, and Solitude:
A Guide for Spiritual Retreat**
by David A. Cooper
This classic guide to meditation and other traditional spiritual
practice is required reading for anyone contemplating a retreat.
Hardcover 0-517-58620-7 1992
Softcover 0-517-88186-1 1994

The Heart of Stillness: The Elements of Spiritual Practice
by David A. Cooper
A comprehensive guidebook
to the basic principles of inner work.
Hardcover 0-517-58621-5 1992
Softcover 0-517-88187-X 1994

One Hundred Graces: Mealtime Blessings
Selected by Marcia and Jack Kelly
A collection from many traditions, beautifully inscribed
in two-color calligraphy.
Hardcover 0-517-58567-7 1992
Softcover 0-517-88230-2 1995

Sanctuaries: The West Coast and Southwest
A Guide to Lodgings in Monasteries, Abbeys, & Retreats of the U.S.
by Marcia and Jack Kelly
The second volume of what *The New York Times* called
"the *Michelin Guide* of the retreat set."
Softcover 0-517-88007-5 1993

Becoming Bread: Meditations on Loving and Transformation
by Gunilla Norris
A book linking the food of the spirit—love—
with the food of the body—bread.
Hardcover 0-517-59168-5 1993

Messengers of the Gods:
Tribal Elders Reveal the Ancient Wisdom of the Earth
by James G. Cowan
A lyrical and visionary attempt to understand the metaphysical
landscape of Northern Australia and the islands just beyond it.
Softcover 0-517-88078-4 1993

Pilgrimage to Dzhvari:
A Woman's Journey of Spiritual Awakening
by Valeria Alfeyeva
An unforgettable introduction to the mystical tradition
of the Eastern Orthodox Church.
Hardcover 0-517-59194-4 1993
Softcover 0-517-88389-9 1995

The Journal of Hildegard of Bingen
by Barbara Lachman
A fictional diary inspired by the life of the twelfth-century
German mystic, abbess, composer, and healer.
Hardcover 0-517-59169-3 1993
Softcover 0-517-88390-2 1995

Sharing Silence: Meditation Practice and Mindful Living
by Gunilla Norris
The essential conditions for meditation and for life itself.
Hardcover 0-517-59506-0 1993

Meditations for the Passages and Celebrations of Life:
A Book of Vigils
by Noela N. Evans
Poignant articulations of the heart's joys and sorrows for
reading at times of renewal or loss.
Hardcover 0-517-59194-4 1994
Softcover 0-517-88299-X 1995

The Alchemy of Illness
by Kat Duff
An exploration of the function and purpose
of illness—approaching it as a spiritual practice.
Softcover 0-517-88097-0 1994

Entering the Sacred Mountain: A Mystical Odyssey
by David A. Cooper
An inspiring chronicle of one man's search for truth in the
traditions of Sufism, Buddhism, and Judaism.
Hardcover 0-517-59653-9 1994

A Walk Between Heaven and Earth:
A Personal Journal on Writing and the Creative Process
by Burghild Nina Holzer
A guide to journal writing in the form of a journal, this book
acts as both inspiration and model.
Softcover 0-517-88096-2 1994

Journeying in Place:
Reflections from a Country Garden
by Gunilla Norris
More meditations on the sacredness of daily experience.
Hardcover 0-517-59762-4 1994

Chant: The Origins, Form, Practice
and Healing Power of Gregorian Chant
by Katharine Le Mée
The companion volume to the phenomenally successful CD.
Hardcover 0-517-70037-9 1994

*Bell Tower books are for sale at your local bookstore, or you may call
1-800-793-BOOK and order with a credit card.*